Practical Guide for the

LITURGY
OF THE
HOURS

Practical Guide for the
LITURGY
OF THE
HOURS

•

Shirley Sullivan

•

Catholic Book Publishing Corp.
New Jersey

NIHIL OBSTAT: Rev. Msgr. Gerard H. McCarren, S.T.D.
   Censor Librorum

IMPRIMATUR: ✠ Most Rev. John J. Myers, J.C.D., D.D.
   Archbishop of Newark

(T-426)

ISBN 978-0-89942-484-2

© 2008 Catholic Book Publishing Corp., NJ
Printed in the U.S.A.

www.catholicbookpublishing.com

CONTENTS

Dedication

For Mary
Mater Thesauri Cordis

PREFACE

ALL people in the Church are invited each day to share in its magnificent prayer, the *Liturgy of the Hours*. In earlier ages this prayer was called the *Divine Office* and constituted a "duty" *(officium)* to be fulfilled by those under religious vows. It was also called the "Breviary." Thus we often encounter the term "Hours" or "Office" to describe different parts of this prayer. In our time this prayer, available in many languages, has become a privilege for all to share. If we decide to adopt this form of prayer, we find two formats available: *Christian Prayer* (Catholic Book Publishing Corp., 1976), a one-volume version and *The Liturgy of the Hours* (Catholic Book Publishing Corp., 1975), a four-volume version. On examination of either format, however, most people become mystified and enthusiasm for this form of prayer may wane. Questions arise: "Here is a collection of wonderful prayers but how are they arranged? How do I start? Where do I start? What is this large section in the middle called the *Psalter*? What are *Evening Prayer I* and *Evening Prayer II*? What prayers do I say when? Help!"

This reaction is quite common and is entirely to be expected. The *Liturgy of the Hours* possesses a difficult and complicated structure. It has a format of prayers that evolved over two millennia and this format cannot be quickly or easily understood. At first this format may confuse those who approach it. But, once understood, the *Liturgy of the Hours* draws the reader into a world of prayer that possesses great and surpassing beauty. We discover the joy of praying in a rich and meaningful way. We also delight to know that in saying the *Liturgy of the Hours*, we join in the same prayer that is being said around the world.

What those who wish to pray the *Liturgy of the Hours* need is a guide. This book hopes to be such a guide. It presents all the various parts of the *Liturgy of the Hours*. For each of the *Hours*, it first offers an outline of the *Hour* and then lays out in detail a sample of that specific *Hour*. In the case of *Morning*, *Evening*, and *Night Prayer*, it also presents the Canticles of Zechariah, Mary, and Simeon. The book begins with a treatment of the two main *Hours* of *Morning* and *Evening Prayer*. It then presents the other *Hours* as well. After the reader has become familiar with all of these, the book introduces the different types of feasts that the Church celebrates and also the special seasons of the Church year.

This book offers guidance to those who may be saying the *Liturgy of the Hours* in private, as an individual form of prayer. It also offers guidance to groups who may be wishing to introduce the *Liturgy of the Hours* as a practice within their parish, showing how the different parts of an *Hour* can be spoken by various members of a group.

This book is based on the two editions of the *Liturgy of the Hours* mentioned above.

GUIDELINES

THIS Practical Guide approaches the *Liturgy of the Hours* as follows:

- Since the human mind understands perplexing material best by first grasping its structure, this *Guide* begins its treatment of each *Hour* with an Outline of that *Hour*.

- The next step in understanding complexity is to practice the structure until it becomes familiar. After the Outline, therefore, this *Guide* presents a practice session for each *Hour*.

- INDIVIDUAL RECITATION: Simply read through the complete *Hour*, reciting **all** the parts.

- GROUP RECITATION: Follow the directions concerning differences in typeface. These are as follows:

LEADER: SAYS WORDS IN BOLD CAPITALS.

Alternate Sides of the Community: Words in Regular Type, lower case.

All the Community: Words in Italic Type, lower case.

- SUGGESTED METHOD: Learn fully one *Hour* and practice it for a week or two. Start with *Morning Prayer* and then add *Evening Prayer*.

- Please note the texts that are frequently used including the *Gloria*, the Invitatory Psalms, and the Canticles of Zechariah and Mary are printed on loose inserts that come with *Christian Prayer* (one-volume version) or the four-volume version.

INTRODUCTION

THE INVITATORY

Christian Prayer (one-volume version)

INDIVIDUAL RECITATION: Recite all parts.

GROUP RECITATION:

LEADER: SAYS WORDS IN BOLD CAPITALS.

Alternate Sides of the Community: Words in Regular Type, lower case.

All the Community: Words in Italic Type, lower case.

OUTLINE

The *Invitatory*, coming from the same root as "invitation" begins the praying of the *Liturgy of the Hours* each day. If *Morning Prayer* is the first part of the *Liturgy of the Hours* prayed on a particular day, it begins with the *Invitatory*. If the *Office of Readings* is the first part of the *Liturgy of the Hours* prayed on a particular day, it begins with the *Invitatory*.

1. The *Invitatory* begins with the prayer:

   LORD, OPEN MY LIPS.

   —And my mouth will proclaim your praise.

2. Second, an Antiphon is given for each day.

3. Third, Psalm 95 is recited.

   • Individual recitation: the Antiphon may be said only at the beginning and the end of Psalm 95.

- Group recitation: the Antiphon is repeated after each verse of Psalm 95.

4. After Psalm 95, the *Gloria* is said. The text is:

GLORY TO THE FATHER, AND TO THE SON, AND TO THE HOLY SPIRIT

As it was in the beginning, is now, and will be forever. Amen.

5. The Antiphon is then repeated.

The pattern, therefore, is as follows:

LORD, OPEN MY LIPS.

—And my mouth will proclaim your praise.

ANTIPHON

[Summary of content of the Psalm in red or bold and italics in Christian Prayer (one-volume version) read silently.]

FIRST LINE OF THE FIRST VERSE OF THE PSALM.

Side One including the Leader: Rest of the first verse of the Psalm.

Side Two: Next verse of the Psalm.

Alternation until the last verse of the Psalm.

GLORY TO THE FATHER, AND TO THE SON, AND TO THE HOLY SPIRIT

As it was in the beginning, is now, and will be forever. Amen.

Antiphon 1 repeated: All together.

PRACTICE

INDIVIDUAL RECITATION: Recite all parts.

GROUP RECITATION:

LEADER: SAYS WORDS IN BOLD CAPITALS.

Alternate Sides of the Community: Words in Regular Type, lower case.

All the Community: Words in Italic Type, lower case.

Sample of *INVITATORY*
Christian Prayer (one-volume version)

Monday, Week I

LORD, OPEN MY LIPS.

—And my mouth will proclaim your praise.

ANTIPHON

LET US APPROACH THE LORD WITH PRAISE AND THANKSGIVING.

Psalm 95

A call to praise God

Encourage each other daily while it is still today (Hebrews 3:13).

COME, LET US SING TO THE LORD
and shout with joy to the Rock who saves us.
Let us approach him with praise and thanksgiving
and sing joyful songs to the Lord.

Let us approach the Lord with praise and thanksgiving.

The Lord is God, the mighty God,
the great king over all the gods.

He holds in his hands the depths of the earth
  and the highest mountains as well.
He made the sea; it belongs to him,
  the dry land, too, for it was formed by his hands.

Let us approach the Lord with praise and thanksgiving.

Come, then, let us bow down and worship,
  bending the knee before the Lord, our maker.
For he is our God and we are his people,
  the flock he shepherds.

Let us approach the Lord with praise and thanksgiving.

Today, listen to the voice of the Lord:
Do not grow stubborn, as your fathers did
  in the wilderness,
When at Meriba and Massah
  they challenged me and provoked me,
Although they had seen all of my works.

Let us approach the Lord with praise and thanksgiving.

Forty years I endured that generation.
I said, "They are a people whose hearts go astray
  and they do not know my ways."
So I swore in my anger,
  "They shall not enter into my rest."

Let us approach the Lord with praise and thanksgiving.

**GLORY TO THE FATHER, AND TO THE
SON, AND TO THE HOLY SPIRIT**

*As it was in the beginning, is now, and will be forever.
  Amen.*

Let us approach the Lord with praise and thanksgiving.

1

MORNING PRAYER
Christian Prayer (one-volume version)

OUTLINE

INDIVIDUAL RECITATION: Recite all parts.

GROUP RECITATION:

LEADER: SAYS WORDS IN BOLD CAPITALS.

Alternate Sides of the Community: Words in Regular Type, lower case.

All the Community: Words in Italic Type, lower case.

OPENING

O GOD, COME TO MY ASSISTANCE.

O Lord, make haste to help me.

Gloria: All together. "Glory to the Father, and to the Son, and to the Holy Spirit,

As it was in the beginning, is now, and will be forever. Amen."

- This opening is omitted if the Invitatory is said.

HYMN

- Chosen from the back of the Volume, as indicated in the Office.

FIRST PSALM

ANTIPHON 1

[Summary of content of the Psalm in red or bold and italics in Christian Prayer (one-volume version) read silently.]

FIRST LINE OF THE FIRST VERSE OF THE PSALM

Side One including the Leader: Rest of the first verse of the Psalm.

Side Two: Next verse of the Psalm.

Alternation until the last verse of the Psalm.

GLORY TO THE FATHER, AND TO THE SON, AND TO THE HOLY SPIRIT

As it was in the beginning, is now, and will be forever. Amen.

PSALM PRAYER

Antiphon 1 repeated: All together.

CANTICLE FROM THE OLD TESTAMENT

ANTIPHON 2

[Summary of content of the Psalm in red or bold and italics in Christian Prayer (one-volume version) read silently.]

FIRST LINE OF THE FIRST VERSE OF THE CANTICLE

Side One including the Leader: Rest of the first verse of the Canticle.

Side Two: Next verse of the Canticle.

Alternation until the last verse of the Canticle.

GLORY TO THE FATHER, AND TO THE SON, AND TO THE HOLY SPIRIT

As it was in the beginning, is now, and will be forever. Amen.

Antiphon 2 repeated: All together.

FINAL PSALM

ANTIPHON 3

[Summary of content of the Psalm in red or bold and italics in Christian Prayer (one-volume version) read silently.]

FIRST LINE OF THE FIRST VERSE OF THE PSALM

Side One including the Leader: Rest of the first verse of the Psalm.

Side Two: Next verse of the Psalm.

Alternation until the last verse of the Psalm.

GLORY TO THE FATHER, AND TO THE SON, AND TO THE HOLY SPIRIT

As it was in the beginning, is now, and will be forever. Amen.

PSALM PRAYER

Antiphon 3 repeated: All together.

READING

- **LEADER**

  or

- Member of the Community

RESPONSORY

FIRST LINE

—First Line

SECOND LINE

—Portion of Second Line

GLORY TO THE FATHER, AND TO THE SON, AND TO THE HOLY SPIRIT.

Repetition of whole First Line.

CANTICLE OF ZECHARIAH

ANTIPHON

FIRST LINE OF CANTICLE

Rest of Canticle: All together

FIRST LINE OF GLORIA

Second line of Gloria: All together.

Antiphon repeated: All together.

INTERCESSIONS

OPENING PRAYER

Response written in italics.

FIRST PRAYER

—Response

Continue in this way to the end of the prayers.

THE LORD'S PRAYER

All together.

FINAL PRAYER

LEADER

DISMISSAL

MAY THE LORD BLESS US, PROTECT US FROM ALL EVIL AND BRING US TO EVERLASTING LIFE.

Amen.

PRACTICE

INDIVIDUAL RECITATION: Recite all parts.

GROUP RECITATION:

LEADER: SAYS WORDS IN BOLD CAPITALS.

Alternate Sides of the Community: Words in Regular Type, lower case.

All the Community: Words in Italic Type, lower case.

MORNING PRAYER
Christian Prayer (one-volume version)
Wednesday, Week IV (page 958)

O GOD, COME TO MY ASSISTANCE.

O Lord, make haste to help me.

Gloria: All together. "Glory to the Father, and to the Son, and to the Holy Spirit,

As it was in the beginning, is now, and will be forever. Amen."

- This opening is omitted if the Invitatory is said.

HYMN

Number 14 or 20 from the back of the Volume.

FIRST PSALM

ANTIPHON 1
MY HEART IS READY, O GOD, MY HEART IS READY.

Psalm 108
Praise of God and a plea for help

Since the Son of God has been exalted above the heavens, his glory is proclaimed through all the earth (Arnobius).

MY HEART IS READY, O GOD;
I will sing, sing your praise.
Awake, my soul;
awake, lyre and harp,
I will awake the dawn.

I will thank you, Lord, among the peoples,
among the nations I will praise you,
for your love reaches to the heavens
and your truth to the skies.
O God, arise above the heavens;
may your glory shine on earth!

O come and deliver your friends;
help with your right hand and reply.
From his holy place God has made this promise:
"I will triumph and divide the land of Shechem,
I will measure out the valley of Succoth.

Gilead is mine and Manasseh,
Ephraim I take for my helmet,
Judah for my commander's staff.
Moab I will use for my washbowl,
on Edom I will plant my shoe.
Over the Philistines I will shout in triumph."

But who will lead me to conquer the fortress?
Who will bring me face to face with Edom?
Will you utterly reject us, O God,
and no longer march with our armies?

Give us help against the foe,
for the help of man is vain.
With God we shall do bravely
and he will trample down our foes.

GLORY TO THE FATHER, AND TO THE SON, AND TO THE HOLY SPIRIT

As it was in the beginning, is now, and will be forever. Amen.

PSALM PRAYER

ACCEPT THE PRAYERS OF YOUR SERVANTS, LORD, AND PREPARE OUR HEARTS TO PRAISE YOUR HOLY NAME. COME TO OUR AID IN TIMES OF TROUBLE, AND MAKE US WORTHY TO SING YOU SONGS OF THANKSGIVING.

Amen.

Antiphon 1

My heart is ready, O God, my heart is ready.

CANTICLE FROM THE OLD TESTAMENT

ANTIPHON 2

THE LORD HAS ROBED ME WITH GRACE AND SALVATION.

Canticle: Isaiah 61:10-62.5

The prophet's joy in the vision of a new Jerusalem

I saw the holy city, new Jerusalem, with the beauty of a bride adorned for her husband. (Revelation 21:2).

I REJOICE HEARTILY IN THE LORD,
in my God is the joy of my soul;
for he has clothed me with a robe of salvation,
and wrapped me in a mantle of justice,
like a bridegroom adorned with a diadem,
like a bride bedecked with her jewels.

As the earth brings forth its plants,
and a garden makes its growth spring up,
so will the Lord God make justice and praise
spring up before all the nations.

For Zion's sake I will not be silent,
for Jerusalem's sake I will not be quiet,
until her vindication shines forth like the dawn
and her victory like a burning torch.

Nations shall behold your vindication,
and all kings your glory;
you shall be called by a new name
pronounced by the mouth of the Lord.
You shall be a glorious crown in the hand of the Lord,
a royal diadem held by your God.

No more shall men call you "Forsaken,"
or your land "Desolate,"
but you shall be called "My delight,"
and your land "Espoused."
For the Lord delights in you,
and makes your land his spouse.

As a young man marries a virgin,
your Builder shall marry you;
and as a bridegroom rejoices in his bride
so shall your God rejoice in you.

GLORY TO THE FATHER, AND TO THE SON, AND TO THE HOLY SPIRIT

As it was in the beginning, is now, and will be forever.
   Amen.

Antiphon 2
The Lord has robed me with grace and salvation.

FINAL PSALM

ANTIPHON 3

I WILL PRAISE MY GOD ALL THE DAYS OF MY LIFE.

Psalm 146

Those who trust in God know what it is to be happy

To praise God in our lives means all we do must be for his glory (Arnobius).

MY SOUL, GIVE PRAISE TO THE LORD;
I will praise the Lord all my days,
make music to my God while I live.

Put no trust in princes,
in mortal men in whom there is no help.
Take their breath, they return to clay
and their plans that day come to nothing.

He is happy who is helped by Jacob's God,
whose hope is in the Lord his God,
who alone made heaven and earth,
the seas and all they contain.

It is he who keeps faith for ever,
who is just to those who are oppressed.
It is he who gives bread to the hungry,
the Lord, who sets prisoners free,

the Lord who gives sight to the blind,
who raises up those who are bowed down,
the Lord, who protects the stranger
and upholds the widow and orphan.

It is the Lord who loves the just

but thwarts the path of the wicked.
The Lord will reign for ever,
Zion's God, from age to age.

GLORY TO THE FATHER, AND TO THE SON, AND TO THE HOLY SPIRIT

As it was in the beginning, is now, and will be forever. Amen.

PSALM PRAYER

GOD OF GLORY AND POWER, THOSE WHO HAVE PUT ALL THEIR TRUST IN YOU ARE HAPPY INDEED. SHINE THE BRIGHTNESS OF YOUR LIGHT ON US, THAT WE MAY LOVE YOU ALWAYS WITH A PURE HEART.

Amen.

Antiphon 3

I will praise my God all the days of my life.

READING   Deuteronomy 4:39-40a

(LEADER or Member of the Community)

Know, and fix in your heart, that the Lord is God in the heavens above and on earth below, and that there is no other. You must keep his statutes and commandments which I enjoin on you today.

RESPONSORY

I WILL BLESS THE LORD ALL MY LIFE LONG.

—*I will bless the Lord all my life long.*

WITH A SONG OF PRAISE EVER ON MY LIPS,

—all my life long.

GLORY TO THE FATHER, AND TO THE SON, AND TO THE HOLY SPIRIT.

I will bless the Lord all my life long.

CANTICLE OF ZECHARIAH

ANTIPHON

LET US SERVE THE LORD IN HOLINESS ALL THE DAYS OF OUR LIFE.

BLESSED BE THE LORD, THE GOD OF ISRAEL,
he has come to his people and set them free.

He has raised up for us a mighty savior,
born of the house of his servant David.

Through his holy prophets he promised of old
   that he would save us from our enemies,
   from the hands of all who hate us.

He promised to show mercy to our fathers
and to remember his holy covenant.

This was the oath he swore to our father Abraham:
to set us free from the hands of our enemies,
free to worship him without fear,
holy and righteous in his sight
   all the days of our life.

You, my child, shall be called the prophet of the
   Most High;

For you will go before the Lord to prepare his way,
to give his people knowledge of salvation
by the forgiveness of their sins.

In the tender compassion of our God
the dawn from on high shall break upon us,
to shine on those who dwell in darkness and the
    shadow of death,
and to guide our feet into the way of peace.

GLORY TO THE FATHER, AND TO THE SON, AND TO THE HOLY SPIRIT

*As it was in the beginning, is now, and will be forever.
    Amen.*

Antiphon

Let us serve the Lord in holiness all the days of our life.

INTERCESSIONS

CHRIST, THE SPLENDOR OF THE FATHER'S GLORY, ENLIGHTENS US WITH HIS WORD. WITH DEEP LOVE WE CALL UPON HIM:

Hear us, King of eternal glory.

BLESSED ARE YOU, THE ALPHA AND THE OMEGA OF OUR FAITH,

—*for you called us out of darkness into your marvelous light.*

YOU ENABLED THE BLIND TO SEE, THE DEAF TO HEAR,

—*help our unbelief.*

LORD, KEEP US IN YOUR LOVE, PRE-SERVE OUR COMMUNITY,

—do not let us become separated from one another.

GIVE US STRENGTH IN TEMPTATION, EN-DURANCE IN TRIAL,

—and gratitude in prosperity.

THE LORD'S PRAYER

All together.

FINAL PRAYER

FATHER, KEEP IN MIND YOUR HOLY COVENANT, SEALED WITH THE BLOOD OF THE LAMB. FORGIVE THE SINS OF YOUR PEOPLE AND LET THIS NEW DAY BRING US CLOSER TO SALVATION.

WE ASK THIS THROUGH OUR LORD JESUS CHRIST, YOUR SON, WHO LIVES AND REIGNS WITH YOU AND THE HOLY SPIRIT, ONE GOD, FOR EVER AND EVER.

Amen.

DISMISSAL

MAY THE LORD BLESS US, PROTECT US FROM ALL EVIL AND BRING US TO EVERLASTING LIFE.

Amen.

2

EVENING PRAYER
Christian Prayer (one-volume version)

OUTLINE

INDIVIDUAL RECITATION: Recite all parts.

GROUP RECITATION:

LEADER: SAYS WORDS IN BOLD CAPITALS.

Alternate Sides of the Community: Words in Regular Type, lower case.

All the Community: Words in Italic Type, lower case.

OPENING

O GOD, COME TO MY ASSISTANCE.

O Lord, make haste to help me.

Gloria: All together. "Glory to the Father, and to the Son, and to the Holy Spirit,

As it was in the beginning, is now, and will be forever. Amen."

- This opening is omitted if the Invitatory is said.

HYMN

- Chosen from the back of the Volume, as indicated in the Office.

FIRST PSALM
ANTIPHON 1

[Summary of content of the Psalm in red or bold and italics in Christian Prayer (one-volume version) read silently.]

FIRST LINE OF THE FIRST VERSE OF THE PSALM.

Side One including the Leader: Rest of the first verse of the Psalm.

Side Two: Next verse of the Psalm.

Alternation until the last verse of the Psalm.

GLORY TO THE FATHER, AND TO THE SON, AND TO THE HOLY SPIRIT

As it was in the beginning, is now, and will be forever. Amen.

PSALM PRAYER

Antiphon 1 repeated: All together.

SECOND PSALM

ANTIPHON 2

[Summary of content of the Psalm in red or bold and italics in Christian Prayer (one-volume version) read silently.]

FIRST LINE OF THE FIRST VERSE OF THE PSALM.

Side One including the Leader: Rest of the first verse of the Psalm.

Side Two: Next verse of the Psalm.

Alternation until the last verse of the Psalm.

GLORY TO THE FATHER, AND TO THE SON, AND TO THE HOLY SPIRIT

As it was in the beginning, is now, and will be forever. Amen.

PSALM PRAYER

Antiphon 2 repeated: All together.

CANTICLE FROM THE NEW TESTAMENT

ANTIPHON 3

FIRST LINE OF THE FIRST VERSE OF THE CANTICLE.

Side One including the Leader: Rest of the first verse of the Canticle.

Side Two: Next verse of the Canticle.

Alternation until the last verse of the Canticle.

GLORY TO THE FATHER, AND TO THE SON, AND TO THE HOLY SPIRIT

As it was in the beginning, is now, and will be forever. Amen.

Antiphon 3 repeated: All together.

READING

- LEADER

  or

- Member of the Community

RESPONSORY

FIRST LINE

—*First Line*

SECOND LINE

—*Portion of Second Line*

GLORY TO THE FATHER, AND TO THE SON, AND TO THE HOLY SPIRIT.

Repetition of whole First Line.

CANTICLE OF MARY

ANTIPHON

FIRST LINE OF CANTICLE

Rest of Canticle: All together.

FIRST LINE OF GLORIA

Second line of Gloria: All together.

Antiphon repeated: All together.

INTERCESSIONS

OPENING PRAYER

Response written in italics.

FIRST PRAYER

　—*Response*

Continue in this way to the end of the prayers.

THE LORD'S PRAYER

All together.

FINAL PRAYER

LEADER

DISMISSAL

MAY THE LORD BLESS US, PROTECT US FROM ALL EVIL AND BRING US TO EVERLASTING LIFE.

Amen.

PRACTICE

INDIVIDUAL RECITATION: Recite all parts.

GROUP RECITATION:

LEADER: SAYS WORDS IN BOLD CAPITALS.

Alternate Sides of the Community: Words in Regular Type, lower case.

All the Community: Words in Italic Type, lower case.

EVENING PRAYER
Christian Prayer (one-volume version)

Thursday, Week II (page 830)

O GOD, COME TO MY ASSISTANCE.

O Lord, make haste to help me.

Gloria: All together. "Glory to the Father, and to the Son, and to the Holy Spirit,

As it was in the beginning, is now, and will be forever. Amen."

- This opening is omitted if the Invitatory is said.

HYMN

Number 45 or 38

FIRST PSALM

ANTIPHON 1

I HAVE MADE YOU THE LIGHT OF ALL NATIONS TO CARRY MY SALVATION TO THE ENDS OF THE EARTH.

Psalm 72

The Messiah's royal power

Opening their treasures, they offered him gifts: gold, frankincense and myrrh. (Matthew 2:11).

I

O GOD, GIVE YOUR JUDGMENT TO THE KING,
to a king's son your justice,
that he may judge your people in justice
and your poor in right judgment.

May the mountains bring forth peace for the people
and the hills, justice.
May he defend the poor of the people
and save the children of the needy
and crush the oppressor.

He shall endure like the sun and the moon
from age to age.
He shall descend like rain on the meadow,
like raindrops on the earth.

In his days justice shall flourish
and peace till the moon fails.
He shall rule from sea to sea,
from the Great River to earth's bounds.

Before him his enemies shall fall,
his foes lick the dust.
The kings of Tarshish and the sea coasts
shall pay him tribute.

The kings of Sheba and Seba
shall bring him gifts.
Before him all kings shall fall prostrate,
all nations shall serve him.

GLORY TO THE FATHER, AND TO THE SON, AND TO THE HOLY SPIRIT

*As it was in the beginning, is now, and will be forever.
Amen.*

Antiphon 1

I have made you the light of all nations to carry my salvation to the ends of the earth.

ANTIPHON 2

THE LORD WILL SAVE THE CHILDREN OF THE POOR AND RESCUE THEM FROM SLAVERY.

II

FOR HE SHALL SAVE THE POOR WHEN THEY CRY

and the needy who are helpless.
He will have pity on the weak
and save the lives of the poor.

From oppression he will rescue their lives,
to him their blood is dear.
Long may he live,
may the gold of Sheba be given him.
They shall pray for him without ceasing
and bless him all the day.

May corn be abundant in the land
to the peaks of the mountains.
May its fruit rustle like Lebanon;
may men flourish in the cities
like grass on the earth.

May his name be blessed for ever
and endure like the sun.

Every tribe shall be blessed in him,
all nations bless his name.

Blessed be the Lord, God of Israel,
who alone works wonders,
ever blessed his glorious name.
Let his glory fill the earth.
Amen! Amen!

GLORY TO THE FATHER, AND TO THE SON, AND TO THE HOLY SPIRIT

As it was in the beginning, is now, and will be forever. Amen.

PSALM PRAYER

WE SHALL CALL UPON YOUR NAME, FATHER, AND PRONOUNCE IT BLESSED ABOVE THE EARTH. GIVE YOUR PEOPLE THE FULLNESS OF PEACE AND JUSTICE IN YOUR KINGDOM.

Amen.

Antiphon 2

The Lord will save the children of the poor and rescue them from slavery.

CANTICLE FROM THE NEW TESTAMENT

ANTIPHON 3

NOW THE VICTORIOUS REIGN OF OUR GOD HAS BEGUN.

Canticle   **Revelation 11: 17-18; 12: 10b-12a**

The judgment of God

WE PRAISE YOU, THE Lord God Almighty,
who is and who was.

You have assumed your great power,
you have begun your reign.

The nations have raged in anger,
but then came your day of wrath
and the moment to judge the dead:
the time to reward your servants the prophets
and the holy ones who revere you,
the great and the small alike.

Now have salvation and power come,
the reign of our God and the authority
of his Anointed One.
For the accuser of our brothers is cast out,
who night and day accused them before God.

They defeated him by the blood of the Lamb
and by the word of their testimony;
love for life did not deter them from death.
So rejoice, you heavens,
and you that dwell therein!

**GLORY TO THE FATHER, AND TO THE
SON, AND TO THE HOLY SPIRIT**

*As it was in the beginning, is now, and will be forever.
    Amen.*

Antiphon 3

Now the victorious reign of our God has begun.

READING   **1 Peter 1:18-23**

(LEADER or Member of the Community)

Realize that you were delivered from the futile
way of life your fathers handed on to you, not by any
diminishable sum of silver or gold, but by Christ's

blood beyond all price: the blood of a spotless, unblemished lamb chosen before the world's foundation and revealed for your sake in these last days. It is through him that you are believers in God, the God who raised him from the dead and gave him glory. Your faith and hope, then, are centered in God.

By obedience to the truth you have purified yourselves for a genuine love of your brothers and sisters; therefore, love one another constantly from the heart. Your rebirth has come, not from a destructible but from an indestructible seed, through the living and enduring word of God.

RESPONSORY

THE LORD IS MY SHEPHERD, I SHALL WANT FOR NOTHING.

—The Lord is my shepherd, I shall want for nothing.

HE HAS BROUGHT ME TO GREEN PASTURES.

—I shall want for nothing.

GLORY TO THE FATHER, AND TO THE SON, AND TO THE HOLY SPIRIT.

The Lord is my shepherd, I shall want for nothing.

CANTICLE OF MARY

ANTIPHON

IF YOU HUNGER FOR HOLINESS, GOD WILL SATISFY YOUR LONGING, GOOD MEASURE, AND FLOWING OVER.

MY SOUL PROCLAIMS THE GREATNESS OF THE LORD,

my spirit rejoices in God my Savior
for he has looked with favor on his lowly servant.

From this day all generations will call me blessed:
the Almighty has done great things for me,
and holy is his Name.

He has mercy on those who fear him
in every generation.

He has shown the strength of his arm,
he has scattered the proud in their conceit.

He has cast down the mighty from their thrones,
and has lifted up the lowly.

He has filled the hungry with good things,
and the rich he has sent away empty.

He has come to the help of his servant Israel
for he has remembered his promise of mercy,
the promise he made to our fathers,
to Abraham and his children for ever.

GLORY TO THE FATHER, AND TO THE SON, AND TO THE HOLY SPIRIT

As it was in the beginning, is now, and will be forever.
Amen.

Antiphon

If you hunger for holiness, God will satisfy your longing,
good measure, and flowing over.

INTERCESSIONS

LIFT UP YOUR HEARTS TO OUR LORD AND SAVIOR WHO GIVES HIS PEOPLE EVERY SPIRITUAL BLESSING. IN THE SPIRIT OF DEVOTION, LET US ASK HIM:

Bless your people, Lord.

MERCIFUL GOD, STRENGTHEN, N., OUR POPE, AND N., OUR BISHOP,

—keep them free from harm.

LOOK FAVORABLY ON OUR COUNTRY, LORD,

—free us from all evil.

CALL MEN TO SERVE AT YOUR ALTAR,

—and to follow you more closely in chastity, poverty and obedience.

TAKE CARE OF YOUR HANDMAIDENS VOWED TO VIRGINITY

—that they may follow you, the divine Lamb, wherever you go.

MAY THE DEAD REST IN ETERNAL PEACE,

—may their union with us be strengthened through the sharing of spiritual goods.

THE LORD'S PRAYER

All together.

FINAL PRAYER

FATHER OF MERCY, HEAR OUR EVENING PRAYER OF PRAISE, AND LET OUR HEARTS NEVER WAVER FROM THE LOVE OF YOUR LAW. LEAD US ON THROUGH NIGHT'S DARKNESS TO THE DAWNING OF ETERNAL LIFE.

WE ASK THIS THROUGH OUR LORD JESUS CHRIST, YOUR SON, WHO LIVES AND REIGNS WITH YOU AND THE HOLY SPIRIT, ONE GOD, FOR EVER AND EVER.

Amen.

DISMISSAL

MAY THE LORD BLESS US, PROTECT US FROM ALL EVIL AND BRING US TO EVERLASTING LIFE.

Amen.

3

DAYTIME PRAYER
**and Proper of the Saints, Commons,
Solemnities, Feasts, Memorials**
Christian Prayer **(one-volume version)**

OUTLINE

INDIVIDUAL RECITATION: Recite all parts.

GROUP RECITATION:

LEADER: SAYS WORDS IN BOLD CAPITALS.

Alternate Sides of the Community: Words in Regular Type, lower case.

All the Community: Words in Italic Type, lower case.

OPENING

O GOD, COME TO MY ASSISTANCE.

O Lord, make haste to help me.

Gloria: All together. "Glory to the Father, and to the Son, and to the Holy Spirit,

As it was in the beginning, is now, and will be forever. Amen."

HYMN

• Chosen from the back of the Volume, as indicated in the Office.

FIRST PSALM

ANTIPHON 1

FIRST LINE OF THE FIRST VERSE OF THE PSALM

Side One including the Leader: Rest of the first verse of the Psalm.

Side Two: Next verse of the Psalm.

Alternation until the last verse of the Psalm.

GLORY TO THE FATHER, AND TO THE SON, AND TO THE HOLY SPIRIT

As it was in the beginning, is now, and will be forever. Amen.

PSALM PRAYER

Antiphon 1 repeated: All together.

SECOND PSALM

ANTIPHON 2

FIRST LINE OF THE FIRST VERSE OF THE PSALM

Side One including the Leader: Rest of the first verse of the Psalm.

Side Two: Next verse of the Psalm.

Alternation until the last verse of the Psalm.

GLORY TO THE FATHER, AND TO THE SON, AND TO THE HOLY SPIRIT

As it was in the beginning, is now, and will be forever. Amen.

PSALM PRAYER

Antiphon 2 repeated: All together.

THIRD PSALM

ANTIPHON 3

FIRST LINE OF THE FIRST VERSE OF THE PSALM

Side One including the Leader: Rest of the first verse of the Psalm.

Side Two: Next verse of the Psalm.

Alternation until the last verse of the Psalm.

GLORY TO THE FATHER, AND TO THE SON, AND TO THE HOLY SPIRIT

As it was in the beginning, is now, and will be forever. Amen.

PSALM PRAYER

Antiphon 3 repeated: All together.

READING

- LEADER
    or
- Member of the Community

RESPONSORY

FIRST LINE
—Second Line

FINAL PRAYER

LEADER

DISMISSAL

LET US PRAISE THE LORD.
And give him thanks.

PRACTICE

INDIVIDUAL RECITATION: Recite all parts.

GROUP RECITATION:

LEADER: SAYS WORDS IN BOLD CAPITALS.

Alternate Sides of the Community: Words in Regular Type, lower case.

All the Community: Words in Italic Type, lower case.

DAYTIME PRAYER
Christian Prayer (one-volume version)
Midmorning, Saturday (page 1022)

OPENING

O GOD, COME TO MY ASSISTANCE.

O Lord, make haste to help me.

Gloria: All together. "Glory to the Father, and to the Son, and to the Holy Spirit,

As it was in the beginning, is now, and will be forever. Amen."

HYMN

- Chosen from the back of the Volume, as indicated in the Office.

FIRST PSALM

ANTIPHON 1

LEAD ME, LORD, IN THE PATH OF YOUR COMMANDMENTS.

Psalm 119:33-40

V (He)

TEACH ME THE DEMANDS OF YOUR PRE-CEPTS

and I will keep them to the end.
Train me to observe your law,
to keep it with my heart.

Guide me in the path of your commands;
for there is my delight.
Bend my heart to your will
and not to love of gain.

Keep my eyes from what is false:
by your word, give me life.
Keep the promise you have made
to the servant who fears you.

Keep me from the scorn I dread,
for your decrees are good.
See, I long for your precepts:
then in your justice, give me life.

GLORY TO THE FATHER, AND TO THE SON, AND TO THE HOLY SPIRIT

As it was in the beginning, is now, and will be forever. Amen.

PSALM PRAYER

IN YOUR JUSTICE GIVE US LIFE, FATHER. DO NOT ALLOW GREED TO POSSESS US BUT INCLINE OUR HEARTS TO YOUR COMMANDS. GIVE US UNDERSTANDING TO KNOW YOUR LAW AND DIRECT US ACCORDING TO YOUR WILL.

Amen.

Antiphon 1

Lead me, Lord, in the path of our commandments.

SECOND PSALM

ANTIPHON 2
THOSE WHO SEEK THE LORD WILL BE FILLED WITH EVERY BLESSING.

Psalm 34

God the savior of the just

You have tasted the sweetness of the Lord (1 Peter 2:3).

I

I WILL BLESS THE LORD AT ALL TIMES,
his praise always on my lips;
in the Lord my soul shall make its boast.
The humble shall hear and be glad.

Glorify the Lord with me.
Together let us praise his name.
I sought the Lord and he answered me;
from all my terrors he set me free.

Look towards him and be radiant;
let your faces not be abashed.
This poor man called, the Lord heard him
and rescued him from all his distress.

The angel of the Lord is encamped
around those who revere him, to rescue them.
Taste and see that the Lord is good.
He is happy who seeks refuge in him.

Revere the Lord, you his saints.
They lack nothing, those who revere him.
Strong lions suffer want and go hungry
but those who seek the Lord lack no blessing.

GLORY TO THE FATHER, AND TO THE SON, AND TO THE HOLY SPIRIT

As it was in the beginning, is now, and will be forever. Amen.

Antiphon 2

Those who seek the Lord will be filled with every blessing.

THIRD PSALM

ANTIPHON 3

SEEK AND STRIVE AFTER PEACE.

II

COME, CHILDREN, AND HEAR ME

that I may teach you the fear of the Lord.
Who is he who longs for life
and many days, to enjoy his prosperity?

Then keep your tongue from evil
and your lips from speaking deceit.
Turn aside from evil and do good;
seek and strive after peace.

The Lord turns his face against the wicked
to destroy their remembrance from the earth.
The Lord turns his eyes to the just
and his ears to their appeal.

They call and the Lord hears
and rescues them in all their distress.
The Lord is close to the broken-hearted;
those whose spirit is crushed he will save.

Many are the trials of the just man
but from them all the Lord will rescue him.

He will keep guard over all his bones,
not one of his bones shall be broken.

Evil brings death to the wicked;
those who hate the good are doomed.
The Lord ransoms the souls of his servants.
Those who hide in him shall not be condemned.

GLORY TO THE FATHER, AND TO THE SON, AND TO THE HOLY SPIRIT

As it was in the beginning, is now, and will be forever. Amen.

PSALM PRAYER

GRACIOUSLY HEAR US, LORD, FOR WE SEEK ONLY YOU. YOU ARE NEAR TO THOSE WHOSE HEART IS RIGHT. OPEN YOURSELF TO ACCEPT OUR SORROWFUL SPIRIT; CALM OUR BODIES AND MINDS WITH THE PEACE WHICH SURPASSES UNDERSTANDING.

Amen.

Antiphon 3

Seek and strive after peace.

READING   1 Kings 8:60-61

(LEADER or Member of the Community)

May all the peoples of the earth know the Lord is God and there is no other. You must be wholly devoted to the Lord, our God, observing his statues and keeping his commandments.

RESPONSORY

LORD, MY GOD, TEACH ME YOUR WAYS.

—Make me live by the light of your truth.

FINAL PRAYER

LET US PRAY.

GOD, ALL-POWERFUL FATHER, FILL YOUR PEOPLE WITH THE LIGHT OF YOUR HOLY SPIRIT, THAT, SAFE FROM EVERY ENEMY, WE MAY REJOICE IN SINGING YOUR PRAISES. GRANT THIS THROUGH CHRIST OUR LORD.

Amen.

DISMISSAL

LET US PRAISE THE LORD.

And give him thanks.

SPECIFIC PARTS AND CELEBRATIONS PROPER OF THE SAINTS, COMMONS, SOLEMNITIES, FEASTS, MEMORIALS

PROPER OF THE SAINTS (page 1060)

- "PROPER": comes from the Latin "proprius," meaning "appropriate" or "suitable."
- The Proper of the Saints contains material that is appropriate to the particular individual whom the Church is celebrating.

- The *Liturgy of the Hours* provides a brief biography of the saint.
- Celebration of the Saints varies. There are four types that we encounter in the *Liturgy of the Hours*.

SOLEMNITY A Solemnity is the highest form of celebration. It is treated like a Sunday. If it falls on a Sunday in Ordinary Time or the Christmas Season, it will replace the Sunday.

- What we say about a solemnity is that "all parts are proper." This means that each part is specially chosen for the celebration. As we pray the celebration, there is minimal of flipping since all we need is right there.
- Let us look at an example: **Annunciation on March 25** (page 1114).
- We find: Evening Prayer I: "all is proper."

  Morning Prayer
  • The Psalms are identical to those of Sunday, Week 1 (page 707).
  • All else is "proper."
  Evening Prayer II: "all is proper."

FEAST A Feast is next in order of a celebration. Feasts, however, are less than a Sunday and do not replace a Sunday. Feasts of the Lord, however, do replace Sundays in Ordinary Time and Sundays of the Christmas Season.

- What we say about a feast is that "only parts are proper." This means that we are going to take some parts of the celebration from elsewhere in the *Liturgy of the Hours*. Where do we get these parts?

COMMONS (page 1355)

- "Commons" comes from the Latin "communis," meaning "common" or "shared."

- The Commons in the *Liturgy of the Hours* contains material that can be used for different celebrations. Thus, for example, there are several Feasts of Our Lady throughout the year. Instead of printing the same material again and again, different feasts use selections from the Common of the Blessed Virgin Mary (page 1368).

- Let us look at this Common. We see that it is complete in itself. We could simply use all of it on any Feast of Our Lady. We see also that within its different sections, there are different choices (see, e.g., page 1371). Our practice will be to choose portions from this Common. How will we know what to choose? We will be directed by the entry for the specific feast we are celebrating.

EXAMPLES OF FEASTS

- Let us now look at the **Birthday of Mary on September 8th** (page 1245).

- We find: No Evening Prayer I.

> Morning Prayer
> All is "proper" except:
> • The Psalms are identical to those of Sunday, Week 1 (page 707).
> • Intercessions are taken from the Common, page 1373.

Evening Prayer
All is "proper" except:
• Psalms are taken from the Common, page 1378.
• Intercessions are taken from the Common, page 1381.

- Let us now look at the **Feast of St. Mark on April 25** (page 1132).
- We find: No Evening Prayer I.

Morning Prayer
All is "proper" except:
• The Psalms are identical to those of Sunday, Week 1 (page 707).

Evening Prayer
All is "proper" except:
• Psalms are taken from the Common of the Apostles, page 1394.

- Let us now look at the **Feast of St. John on December 27** (page 1347).
- We find: No Evening Prayer I.

Morning Prayer
All is "proper" except:
• The Psalms are identical to those of Sunday, Week 1 (page 707).

Evening Prayer
• All is taken from Evening Prayer II of Christmas Day, (page 147).

MEMORIALS

- A Memorial is next in order of celebration. In the
case of Memorials most of the material will come
from an appropriate Common. There may be
some parts of the celebration that are proper.
The Final Prayer is normally proper.

St. Thomas Aquinas, January 28 (page 1075).

Morning Prayer

• Psalms and Antiphons from the Weekday.
• Hymn, Reading, Responsory and Intercessions
either from the Weekday or the Common of
Doctors (page 1435).
• Antiphon for the Canticle of Zechariah and the
Final Prayer from the Proper.

Evening Prayer
Follow the same pattern as for Morning Prayer
except:
• Antiphon for the Canticle of Mary and the Final
Prayer from the Proper.

St. Catherine of Siena, April 29 (page 1136).

Morning Prayer

• Psalms and Antiphons from the Easter Weekday.
• Hymn, Reading, Responsory and Intercessions
either from Easter Weekday or the Common of
Virgins (page 1441).
• Antiphon for the Canticle of Zechariah and the
Final Prayer from the Proper.

Evening Prayer
Follow the same pattern as for Morning Prayer
except:

• Antiphon for the Canticle of Mary and the Final Prayer from the Proper.

St. Benedict, July 11 (page 1191).

Morning Prayer
• Psalms and Antiphons from the Weekday.
• Hymn, Reading, Responsory and Intercessions either from the Weekday or the Common of Holy Men: Religious (page 1470).
• Antiphon for the Canticle of Zechariah and the Final Prayer from the Proper.

Evening Prayer
Follow the same pattern as for Morning Prayer except:
• Antiphon for the Canticle of Mary and the Final Prayer from the Proper.

St. Clare, August 11 (page 1224).

Morning Prayer
• Psalms and Antiphons from the Weekday.
• Hymn, Reading, Responsory, Antiphon for the Canticle of Zechariah and Intercessions either from the Weekday or the Common of Virgins (page 1441).
• Final Prayer from the Proper.

Evening Prayer
Follow the same pattern as for Morning Prayer except:
• Antiphon for the Canticle of Mary either from the Weekday or the Common of Virgins (page 1441).
• Final Prayer from the Proper.

Our Lady of Sorrows, September 15 (page 1260).

Morning Prayer
All is "proper" except:
• The Psalms are identical to those of Sunday, Week 1 (page 707).
• Intercessions are taken from the Common, page 1373.

Evening Prayer
All is "proper" except:
• Psalms are taken from the Common, page 1378.
• Intercessions are taken from the Common, page 1381.

St. Teresa of Avila, October 15 (page 1289).

Morning Prayer
• Psalms and Antiphons from the Weekday.
• Hymn, Reading, Responsory, Antiphon for the Canticle of Zechariah and Intercessions either from the Weekday or the Common of Virgins (page 1441).
• Final Prayer from the Proper.

Evening Prayer
Follow the same pattern as for Morning Prayer except:
• Antiphon for the Canticle of Mary either from the Weekday or the Common of Virgins (page 1441).
• Final Prayer from the Proper.

St. Francis Xavier, December 3 (page 1329).

Morning Prayer
• Psalms and Antiphons from the Weekday.

• Hymn, Reading, Responsory, Antiphon for the Canticle of Zechariah and Intercessions either from the Weekday or the Common of Pastors (page 1426).

• Final Prayer from the Proper.

Evening Prayer
Follow the same pattern as for Morning Prayer except:

• Antiphon for the Canticle of Mary either from the Weekday or the Common of Pastors (page 1426).

• Final Prayer from the Proper.

OPTIONAL MEMORIALS

• These are celebrations that can be chosen or omitted.

• They may be chosen, for example, if a church is named after a saint or if the saint is very popular in a particular place or country.

• The pattern for celebration is the same as that of Memorials.

GENERAL ROMAN CALENDAR (page 22)

Memorials are listed in regular type.

SOLEMNITIES are listed in BOLD CAPITALS.

FEASTS are listed in REGULAR CAPITALS.

Optional Memorials are listed in *italics*. No ranking is given to them in the right column.

PSALMS FOR MORNING PRAYER OF FEAST DAYS

- These Psalms are always chosen from Sunday Week 1 (page 707).
- The Psalms, numbers 63 and 149, are said in the usual way.
- The Old Testament Canticle is from the Book of Daniel.
- In private recitation, this Canticle is said in the usual way. The Gloria is not said because it has been incorporated into the last lines of the Canticle.
- In group recitation, the pattern for saying this Canticle is as follows.

CANTICLE FROM DANIEL

LEADER (L): SAYS WORDS IN BOLD CAPITALS.

Side 1 = (S 1)

Side 2 = (S 2)

STANZA 1

(L) BLESS THE LORD, ALL YOU WORKS OF THE LORD.

(S 1) Praise and exalt him above all forever.

(S 1) Angels of the Lord,

(S 2) bless the Lord.

(S 1) You heavens,

(S 2) bless the Lord.

(S 1) All you waters above the heavens,

(S 2) bless the Lord.

(S 1) All you hosts of the Lord,

(S 2) bless the Lord.

(S 1) Sun and moon,

(S 2) bless the Lord.

(S 1) Stars of heaven,

(S 2) bless the Lord.

STANZA 2

(S 2) Every shower and dew,

(S 1) bless the Lord.

(S 2) All you winds,

(S 1) bless the Lord.

(S 2) Fire and heat,

(S 1) bless the Lord.

(S 2) Cold and chill,

(S 1) bless the Lord.

(S 2) Dew and rain,

(S 1) bless the Lord.

(S 2) Frost and chill,

(S 1) bless the Lord.

(S 2) Ice and snow,

(S 1) bless the Lord.

(S 2) Nights and days,

(S 1) bless the Lord.

(S 2) Light and darkness,

(S 1) bless the Lord.

(S 2) Lightnings and clouds,

(S 1) bless the Lord.

STANZA 3

(S 1) Let the earth bless the Lord.

(S 2) Praise and exalt him above all forever.

(S 1) Mountains and hills,

(S 2) bless the Lord.

(S 1) Everything growing from the earth,

(S 2) bless the Lord.

(S 1) You springs,

(S 2) bless the Lord.

(S 1) Seas and rivers,

(S 2) bless the Lord.

(S 1) You dolphins and all water creatures,

(S 2) bless the Lord.

(S 1) All you birds of the air,

(S 2) bless the Lord.

(S 1) All you beasts, wild and tame,

(S 2) bless the Lord.

(S 1) You sons of men,

(S 2) bless the Lord.

STANZA 4

(S 2) O Israel, bless the Lord.

(S 1) Praise and exalt him above all forever.

(S 2) Priests of the Lord,

(S 1) bless the Lord.

(S 2) Servants of the Lord,

(S 1) bless the Lord.

(S 2) Spirits and souls of the just,

(S 1) bless the Lord.

(S 2) Holy men of humble heart,

(S 1) bless the Lord.

(S 2) Hananiah, Azariah, Mishael, bless the Lord.

(S 1) Praise and exalt him above all forever.

STANZA 5

(S 1) Let us bless the Father, and the son, and the Holy Spirit.

(S 2) Let us praise and exalt him above all forever.

(S 1) Blessed are you, Lord, in the firmament of heavens.

(S 2) Praiseworthy and glorious and exalted above all forever.

4

NIGHT PRAYER
and
Seasons of the Church Year
Christian Prayer (one-volume version)

OUTLINE

INDIVIDUAL RECITATION: Recite all parts.

GROUP RECITATION:

LEADER: SAYS WORDS IN BOLD CAPITALS.

Alternate Sides of the Community: Words in Regular Type, lower case.

All the Community: Words in Italic Type, lower case.

OPENING

O GOD, COME TO MY ASSISTANCE.

O Lord, make haste to help me.

Gloria: All together. "Glory to the Father, and to the Son, and to the Holy Spirit,

As it was in the beginning, is now, and will be forever. Amen."

1. Brief examination of conscience followed by a prayer of forgiveness.

2. Hymn.

FIRST PSALM

ANTIPHON 1

[Summary of content of the Psalm in red or bold and italics in Christian Prayer (one-volume version) read silently.]

FIRST LINE OF THE FIRST VERSE OF THE PSALM.

Side One including the Leader: Rest of the first verse of the Psalm.

Side Two: Next verse of the Psalm.

Alternation until the last verse of the Psalm.

GLORY TO THE FATHER, AND TO THE SON, AND TO THE HOLY SPIRIT

As it was in the beginning, is now, and will be forever. Amen.

PSALM PRAYER

Antiphon 1 repeated: All together.

SECOND PSALM (when appropriate)

ANTIPHON 2

[Summary of content of the Psalm in red and italics in Christian Prayer (one-volume version) read silently.]

FIRST LINE OF THE FIRST VERSE OF THE PSALM.

Side One including the Leader: Rest of the first verse of the Psalm.

Side Two: Next verse of the Psalm.

Alternation until the last verse of the Psalm.

GLORY TO THE FATHER, AND TO THE SON, AND TO THE HOLY SPIRIT

As it was in the beginning, is now, and will be forever. Amen.

PSALM PRAYER

Antiphon 2 repeated: All together.

READING

- LEADER
    or
- Member of the Community

RESPONSORY

FIRST LINE
  —*Second Line*
THIRD LINE
  —*Fourth Line*
GLORY TO THE FATHER, AND TO THE SON, AND TO THE HOLY SPIRIT.
Repeat First Line: All together.

CANTICLE OF SIMEON

ANTIPHON

FIRST LINE OF CANTICLE
Rest of Canticle: All together.

FIRST LINE OF GLORIA
Second line of Gloria: All together.
Antiphon repeated: All together.

FINAL PRAYER

LEADER

CONCLUSION

LEADER: May the all-powerful Lord grant us a restful night and a peaceful death.
Amen.

ANTIPHON IN HONOR OF THE BLESSED VIRGIN
- Choose from selection given.

PRACTICE

INDIVIDUAL RECITATION: Recite all parts.

GROUP RECITATION:

LEADER: SAYS WORDS IN BOLD CAPITALS.

Alternate Sides of the Community: Words in Regular Type, lower case.

All the Community: Words in Italic Type, lower case.

NIGHT PRAYER
Christian Prayer (one-volume version)
Sunday after Evening Prayer 1 (page 1034)

OPENING

O GOD, COME TO MY ASSISTANCE.

O Lord, make haste to help me.

Gloria: All together. "Glory to the Father, and to the Son, and to the Holy Spirit,

As it was in the beginning, is now, and will be forever. Amen."

1. Brief examination of conscience followed by a prayer of forgiveness.

2. Hymn.

FIRST PSALM

ANTIPHON 1

HAVE MERCY, LORD, AND HEAR MY PRAYER.

Psalm 4

Thanksgiving

The resurrection of Christ was God's supreme and wholly marvelous work (Saint Augustine).

WHEN I CALL, ANSWER ME, O GOD OF JUSTICE;

from anguish you released me, have mercy and hear me!

O men, how long will your hearts be closed,
will you love what is futile and seek what is false?

It is the Lord who grants favors to those whom he loves;
the Lord hears me whenever I call him.

Fear him; do not sin: ponder on your bed and be still.
Make justice your sacrifice and trust in the Lord.

"What can bring us happiness?" many say.
Let the light of your face shine on us, O Lord.

You have put into my heart a greater joy
than they have from abundance of corn and new wine.

I will lie down in peace and sleep comes at once
for you alone, Lord, make me dwell in safety.

GLORY TO THE FATHER, AND TO THE SON, AND TO THE HOLY SPIRIT

As it was in the beginning, is now, and will be forever. Amen.

Antiphon 1

Have mercy, Lord, and hear my prayer.

SECOND PSALM (when appropriate)

ANTIPHON 2

IN THE SILENT HOURS OF NIGHT, BLESS THE LORD.

Psalm 134

Evening Prayer in the Temple

Praise our God, all you his servants, you who fear him, small and great (Revelation 19:5).

O COME, BLESS THE LORD,
all you who serve the Lord,
who stand in the house of the Lord,
in the courts of the house of our God.

Lift up your hands to the holy place
and bless the Lord through the night.

May the Lord bless you from Zion,
he who made both heaven and earth.

GLORY TO THE FATHER, AND TO THE SON, AND TO THE HOLY SPIRIT

As it was in the beginning, is now, and will be forever. Amen.

Antiphon 2

In the silent hours of night, bless the Lord.

READING

(LEADER or Member of the Community)

Hear, O Israel! The Lord is our God, the Lord alone! Therefore, you shall love the Lord, your God, with all your heart, and with all your soul, and with all your strength. Take to heart these words which I enjoin on you today. Drill them into your children. Speak of them at home and abroad, whether you are busy or at rest.

RESPONSORY

INTO YOUR HANDS, LORD, I COMMEND MY SPIRIT.

—Into your hands, Lord, I commend my spirit.

YOU HAVE REDEEMED US, LORD GOD OF TRUTH.

—I commend my spirit.

GLORY TO THE FATHER, AND TO THE SON, AND TO THE HOLY SPIRIT.

Into your hands, Lord, I commend my spirit.

CANTICLE OF SIMEON

ANTIPHON

PROTECT US, LORD, AS WE STAY AWAKE; WATCH OVER US AS WE SLEEP, THAT AWAKE, WE MAY KEEP WATCH WITH CHRIST, AND ASLEEP, REST IN HIS PEACE.

GOSPEL CANTICLE Luke 2:29-32

Christ is the light of the nations and the glory of Israel

LORD, NOW YOU LET YOUR SERVANT GO IN PEACE;
Your word has been fulfilled:

My own eyes have seen the salvation
Which you have prepared in the sight of every people;

A light to reveal you to the nations
And the glory of your people Israel.

GLORY TO THE FATHER, AND TO THE SON, AND TO THE HOLY SPIRIT

As it was in the beginning, is now, and will be forever. Amen.

Antiphon

Protect us, Lord, as we stay awake; watch over us as we sleep, that awake, we may keep watch with Christ, and asleep, rest in his peace.

FINAL PRAYER

LET US PRAY.

LORD, BE WITH US THROUGHOUT THIS NIGHT. WHEN DAY COMES MAY WE RISE FROM SLEEP TO REJOICE IN THE RESURRECTION OF YOUR CHRIST, WHO LIVES AND REIGNS FOR EVER AND EVER.

Amen.

CONCLUSION

MAY THE ALL-POWERFUL LORD GRANT US A RESTFUL NIGHT AND A PEACE-FUL DEATH.

Amen.

ANTIPHON IN HONOR OF THE BLESSED VIRGIN

Loving mother of the Redeemer,
gate of heaven, star of the sea,
assist your people who have fallen yet strive to rise again.
To the wonderment of nature you bore your Creator,

yet remained a virgin after as before.
You who received Gabriel's joyful greeting,
have pity on us poor sinners.

SEASONS OF THE CHURCH YEAR

STRUCTURE OF THE YEAR

Advent

Christmas Season

A Portion of Ordinary Time

Lent

Easter up until Pentecost

Remainder of Ordinary Time

ORDINARY TIME

Sundays 1-9 (page 245)

Sundays 7-34 (page 611)

- The first portion of Ordinary time begins after the end of the Christmas Season.
- The number of Sundays during this portion of Ordinary Time depends on when Lent begins.
- Ordinary Time resumes on the Monday after the Sunday of **Pentecost**. The First Sunday after Pentecost is the Solemnity of the **Holy Trinity**, the Second Sunday after Pentecost is the Solemnity of **The Body and Blood of Christ**

(**Corpus Christi**). The Friday after Corpus Christ is the Solemnity of the **Sacred Heart**.

• How do we know when to change back to Ordinary Time? We need to consult: **Principal Celebrations of the Liturgical Year** (page 20).

Features of Ordinary Time

• Sundays always have portions that are proper.
• Example of a **Sunday: Second Sunday in Ordinary Time** (page 246)

Top Right Entry: indicates the Week of the Psalter to use.

Evening Prayer I (Saturday)
All as in Psalter except:
• The Antiphon for the Canticle of Mary and the Final Prayer are proper.
Morning Prayer
All as in Psalter except:
• The Antiphon for the Canticle of Zechariah and the Final Prayer are proper.
Evening Prayer II (Sunday)
All as in Psalter except:
• The Antiphon for the Canticle of Mary and the Final Prayer are proper.
Weekdays will follow the Psalter except when there is a Solemnity, Feast or Memorial.

ADVENT

Sundays

Evening Prayer I (Saturday)
All is proper except:

• The Psalms are taken from the appropriate week of the Psalter.

Morning Prayer
All is proper except:
• The Psalms are taken from the appropriate week of the Psalter.

Evening Prayer II (Sunday)
All is proper except:
• The Psalms are taken from the appropriate week of the Psalter.

Mondays to Saturdays

Morning Prayer
• All is as in the appropriate week of the Psalter up to the end of the Psalms. Then all is proper.

Evening Prayer
• All is as in the appropriate week of the Psalter up to the end of the Psalms. Then all is proper.

CHRISTMAS

Sundays and Special Feasts

Christmas Day, December 25

Feast of the Holy Family (Sunday within the Octave of Christmas)

Solemnity of Mary, Mother of God, January 1

Second Sunday after Christmas

Epiphany

Baptism of the Lord

Evening Prayer I
All is proper.

Morning Prayer
All is proper.

Evening Prayer II
All is proper.

Mondays to Saturdays

From the Solemnity of Mary until the Baptism of the Lord please refer to pages 53-58 to pray the saints' feast days.

LENT

Ash Wednesday to Saturday (first 4 days of Lent)

Morning Prayer
• All is as in Psalter Week IV up to the end of the Psalms. Then all is proper.

Evening Prayer
• All is as in Psalter Week IV up to the end of the Psalms. Then all is proper.

Sundays

Evening Prayer I
All is proper except:
• The Psalms are taken from the appropriate week of the Psalter.

Morning Prayer
All is proper except:
• The Psalms are taken from the appropriate week of the Psalter.

Evening Prayer II
All is proper except:
• The Psalms are taken from the appropriate week of the Psalter.

Mondays to Saturdays

Morning Prayer
• All is as in the appropriate week of the Psalter up to the end of the Psalms. Then all is proper.

Evening Prayer
• All is as in the appropriate week of the Psalter up to the end of the Psalms. Then all is proper.

EASTER SEASON UNTIL PENTECOST

Easter Sunday

Morning Prayer
• All is proper.

Evening Prayer
• All is proper.

Octave of Easter

Morning Prayer
• All as on Easter Sunday up to the end of the Psalms. Then all is proper.

Evening Prayer
• All as on Easter Sunday up to the end of the Psalms. Then all is proper.

Remaining Sundays of Easter

Evening Prayer I
All is proper except:
• The Psalms are taken from the appropriate week of the Psalter.

Morning Prayer
All is proper except:
• The Psalms are taken from the appropriate week of the Psalter.

Evening Prayer II

All is proper except:

• The Psalms are taken from the appropriate week of the Psalter.

Mondays to Saturdays

Morning Prayer

• All is as in the appropriate week of the Psalter up to the end of the Psalms. Then all is proper.

Evening Prayer

• All is as in the appropriate week of the Psalter up to the end of the Psalms. Then all is proper.

Solemnities of Ascension and Pentecost

Evening Prayer I

• All is proper.

Morning Prayer

• All is proper.

Evening Prayer II

• All is proper.

5

OFFICE OF READINGS
The Liturgy of the Hours
(four-volume version)

OUTLINE

INDIVIDUAL RECITATION: Recite all parts.

GROUP RECITATION:

LEADER: SAYS WORDS IN BOLD CAPITALS.

Alternate Sides of the Community: Words in Regular Type, lower case.

All the Community: Words in Italic Type, lower case.

OPENING

If the *Office of Readings* is the first part of the *Liturgy of the Hours* prayed on a particular day, it begins with the *Invitatory*. At all other times:

O GOD, COME TO MY ASSISTANCE.

O Lord, make haste to help me.

Gloria: All together. "Glory to the Father, and to the Son, and to the Holy Spirit,

As it was in the beginning, is now, and will be forever. Amen."

HYMN

• As indicated in the Office.

FIRST PSALM

ANTIPHON 1

[Summary of content of the Psalm in red or bold and italics in Christian Prayer (one-volume version) read silently.]

FIRST LINE OF THE FIRST VERSE OF THE PSALM

Side One including the Leader: Rest of the first verse of the Psalm.

Side Two: Next verse of the Psalm.

Alternation until the last verse of the Psalm.

GLORY TO THE FATHER, AND TO THE SON, AND TO THE HOLY SPIRIT

As it was in the beginning, is now, and will be forever. Amen.

Antiphon 1 repeated: All together.

SECOND PSALM
ANTIPHON 2

[Summary of content of the Psalm in red and italics in Christian Prayer (one-volume version) read silently.]

FIRST LINE OF THE FIRST VERSE OF THE PSALM

Side One including the Leader: Rest of the first verse of the Psalm.

Side Two: Next verse of the Psalm.

Alternation until the last verse of the Psalm.

GLORY TO THE FATHER, AND TO THE SON, AND TO THE HOLY SPIRIT

As it was in the beginning, is now, and will be forever. Amen.

Antiphon 2 repeated: All together.

THIRD PSALM
ANTIPHON 3

[Summary of content of the Psalm in red and italics in Christian Prayer (one-volume version) read silently.]

FIRST LINE OF THE FIRST VERSE OF THE PSALM

Side One including the Leader: Rest of the first verse of the Psalm.

Side Two: Next verse of the Psalm.

Alternation until the last verse of the Psalm.

GLORY TO THE FATHER, AND TO THE SON, AND TO THE HOLY SPIRIT

As it was in the beginning, is now, and will be forever. Amen.

PSALM PRAYER

Antiphon 3 repeated: All together.

RESPONSORY

FIRST LINE

—Second Line

FIRST READING

- **LEADER**

    or

- Member of the Community

RESPONSORY

FIRST LINE

—Second Line

THIRD LINE

—Fourth Line (repetition of Second Line).

SECOND READING

- **LEADER**

    or

- Member of the Community.

RESPONSORY

FIRST LINE
—*Second Line*

THIRD LINE
—*Fourth Line (repeat of Second Line)*

TE DEUM
(On Sundays, except in Lent, and on Feasts and Solemnities.)

FINAL PRAYER

LEADER

PRACTICE

OFFICE OF READINGS
The Liturgy of the Hours (four-volume version)
Wednesday, Week III
FEAST OF ST. AUGUSTINE OF HIPPO August 28

INDIVIDUAL RECITATION: Recite all parts.

GROUP RECITATION:

LEADER: SAYS WORDS IN BOLD CAPITALS.

Alternate Sides of the Community: Words in Regular Type, lower case.

All the Community: Words in Italic Type, lower case.

OPENING

If the *Office of Readings* is the first part of the *Liturgy of the Hours* prayed on a particular day, it begins with the *Invitatory*. At all other times:

O GOD, COME TO MY ASSISTANCE.

O Lord, make haste to help us.

Gloria: "Glory to the Father, and to the Son, and to the Holy Spirit,

As it was in the beginning, is now, and will be forever. Amen."

HYMN

- As indicated in the Office.

FIRST PSALM

ANTIPHON 1

WHEREVER YOU ARE, LORD, THERE IS MERCY, THERE IS TRUTH.

Psalm 89: 2-38

God's favors to the house of David

According to his promise, the Lord has raised up Jesus, a Savior, from the family of David (Acts 13:22, 23).

I

I WILL SING FOR EVER OF YOUR LOVE, O LORD;

through all ages my mouth will proclaim your truth.
Of this I am sure, that your love lasts for ever,
that your truth is firmly established as the heavens.

"With my chosen one I have made a covenant;
I have sworn to David my servant:
I will establish your dynasty for ever
and set up your throne through all ages."

The heavens proclaim your wonders, O Lord;
the assembly of your holy ones proclaims your truth.
For who in the skies can compare with the Lord
or who is like the Lord among the sons of God?

A God to be feared in the council of the holy ones,
great and dreadful to all around him.
O Lord God of hosts, who is your equal?
You are mighty, O Lord, and truth is your garment.

It is you who rule the sea in its pride;
it is you who still the surging of its waves.
You crushed the monster Rahab and killed it,
scattering your foes with your mighty arm.

The heavens are yours, the world is yours.
It is you who founded the earth and all it holds;
it is you who created the North and the South.
Tabor and Hermon shout with joy at your name.

Yours is a mighty arm, O Lord;
your hand is strong, your right hand ready.
Justice and right are the pillars of your throne,
love and truth walk in your presence.

Happy the people who acclaim such a king,
who walk, O Lord, in the light of your face,
who find their joy every day in your name,
who make your justice the source of their bliss.

For you, O Lord, are the glory of their strength;
by your favor it is that our might is exalted:
for our ruler is in the keeping of the Lord;
our king in the keeping of the Holy One of Israel.

GLORY TO THE FATHER, AND TO THE SON, AND TO THE HOLY SPIRIT

As it was in the beginning, is now, and will be forever. Amen.

Antiphon

Wherever you are, Lord, there is mercy, there is truth.

SECOND PSALM

ANTIPHON 2

WHEN THE SON OF GOD CAME INTO THIS WORLD, HE WAS BORN OF DAVID'S LINE.

II

OF OLD YOU SPOKE IN A VISION.
To your friends the prophets you said:
"I have set the crown on a warrior,
I have exalted one chosen from the people.

I have found David my servant
and with my holy oil anointed him.
My hand shall always be with him
and my arm shall make him strong.

The enemy shall never outwit him
nor the evil man oppress him.
I will beat down his foes before him
and smite those who hate him.

My truth and my love shall be with him;
by my name his might shall be exalted.
I will stretch out his hand to the Sea
and his right hand as far as the River.

He will say to me: 'You are my father,
my God, the rock who saves me.'
And I will make him my first-born,
the highest of the kings of the earth.

I will keep my love for him always;
with him my covenant shall last.
I will establish his dynasty for ever,
make his throne endure as the heavens.

GLORY TO THE FATHER, AND TO THE SON, AND TO THE HOLY SPIRIT

As it was in the beginning, is now, and will be forever. Amen.

Antiphon

When the Son of God came into this world, he was born of David's line.

THIRD PSALM

ANTIPHON 3

ONCE FOR ALL I SWORE TO MY SERVANT DAVID; HIS DYNASTY SHALL NEVER FAIL.

III

"IF HIS SONS FORSAKE MY LAW
and refuse to walk as I decree
and if ever they violate my statutes,
refusing to keep my commands;

then I will punish their offenses with the rod,
then I will scourge them on account of their guilt.
But I will never take back my love,
my truth will never fail.

I will never violate my covenant
nor go back on the word I have spoken.
Once for all, I have sworn by my holiness.
'I will never lie to David.

His dynasty shall last for ever.
In my sight his throne is like the sun;
like the moon, it shall endure for ever,
a faithful witness in the skies.' "

GLORY TO THE FATHER, AND TO THE SON, AND TO THE HOLY SPIRIT

As it was in the beginning, is now, and will be forever. Amen.

PSALM PRAYER

GOD, YOU ANOINTED YOUR SERVANT JESUS WITH HOLY OIL AND RAISED HIM HIGHER THAN ALL KINGS ON EARTH. IN THIS YOU FULFILLED THE PROMISE MADE TO DAVID'S DESCENDANTS AND ESTABLISHED A LASTING COVENANT THROUGH YOUR FIRST-BORN SON. DO NOT FORGET YOUR HOLY COVENANT, SO THAT WE WHO ARE SIGNED WITH THE BLOOD OF YOUR SON THROUGH THE NEW SACRAMENT OF FAITH MAY SING OF YOUR MERCIES FOREVER.

Amen.

Antiphon

Once for all I swore to my servant David: his dynasty shall never fail.

RESPONSORY

When we listen to your word, our minds are filled with light.

—*It is the lowly heart that understands.*

FIRST READING

(LEADER or Member of the Community)

From the Letter to the Philippians 3: 3-16

It is we who are the circumcision, who worship in the spirit of God and glory in Christ Jesus rather than putting our trust in the flesh—though I can be confident even there. If anyone thinks he has a right to put his trust in external evidence, all the more can I! I was circumcised on the eighth day, being of the stock of Israel and the tribe of Benjamin, a Hebrew of Hebrew origins; in legal observance I was a Pharisee, and so zealous that I persecuted the church. I was above reproach when it came to justice based on the law.

But those things I used to consider gain I have now reappraised as loss in the light of Christ. I have come to rate all as loss in the light of the surpassing knowledge of my Lord Jesus Christ. For his sake I have forfeited everything; I have accounted all else rubbish so that Christ may be my wealth and I may be in him, not having any justice of my own based on observance of the law. The justice I possess is that which comes through faith in Christ. It has its origin in God and is based on faith. I wish to know Christ and the power flowing from his resurrection; likewise to know how to share in his sufferings by being formed into the pattern of his death. Thus do I hope that I may arrive at resurrection from the dead.

It is not that I have reached it yet, or have already finished my course; but I am racing to grasp the prize if possible, since I have been grasped by Christ [Jesus]. Brothers, I do not think of myself as having reached the finish line. I give no thought to what lies behind but push on to what is ahead. My entire attention is on the finish line as I run toward the prize to which God calls me—life on high in Christ Jesus. All of us who are spiritually mature must have this attitude. If you see it another way, God will clarify the difficulty for you. It is important that we continue on our course, no matter what stage we have reached.

RESPONSORY

I HAVE COUNTED ALL THINGS WORTH-LESS SO THAT I MIGHT GAIN CHRIST.

—*I wish to know Christ and the power of his resurrection, and to be one with him in his sufferings.*

WE BELIEVE THAT IF WE DIE WITH CHRIST, WE SHALL ALSO LIVE WITH HIM.

—*I wish to know Christ and the power of his resurrection, and to be one with him in his sufferings.*

SECOND READING

Confessions of St. Augustine, Book 7, 10, 18; 10, 27 (page 1355)

Urged to reflect upon myself, I entered under your guidance into the inmost depth of my soul. I was able to do so because you were my helper. On entering into myself I saw, as it were with the eye of the soul, what was beyond the eye of the soul, beyond my spirit: your immutable Light. It was not the ordinary light perceptible to all flesh, nor was it merely something of greater magnitude but still essentially akin, shining more clearly and diffusing itself everywhere by its intensity. No, it was something entirely distinct, something altogether different from all these things; and it did not rest above my mind as oil on the surface of water, nor was it above me as heaven is above earth. This light was above me because it had made me; I was below it because I was created by it. He who has come to know the truth knows this light.

O eternal truth, true love and beloved eternity. You are my God. To you do I sigh day and night.

When I first came to know you, you drew me to yourself so that I might see that there were things for me to see, but that I myself was not yet ready to see them. Meanwhile you overcame the weakness of my vision, sending forth most strongly the beams of your light, and I trembled at once with love and dread. I learned that I was in a region unlike yours and far distant from you, and I thought I heard your voice from on high: "I am the food of grown men; grow then and you will feed on me. Nor will you change me into yourself like bodily food, but you will be changed into me."

I sought a way to gain the strength which I needed to enjoy you. But I did not find it until I embraced the mediator between God and men, the man Christ Jesus, who is above all, God blessed forever. He was calling me and saying; I am the way of truth, I am the life. He was offering the food which I lacked the strength to take, the food he had mingled with our flesh. For the Word became flesh, that your wisdom, by which you created all things, might provide milk for us children.

Late have I loved you, O Beauty ever ancient, ever new, late have I loved you! You were within me, but I was outside, and it was there that I searched for you. In my unloveliness I plunged into the lovely things which you created. You were with me, but I was not with you. Created things kept me from you; yet if they had not been in you, they would not have been at all. You called, you shouted, and you broke through my deafness. You flashed, you shone, and you dispelled my blindness. You breathed your fragrance on me; I drew in breath and now I pant for you. I have tasted you, now I hunger and thirst for more. You touched me, and I burned for your peace.

RESPONSORY

O TRUTH, YOU ARE THE LIGHT OF MY HEART.

LET YOUR LIGHT SPEAK TO ME, NOT MY OWN DARKNESS.

I WENT ASTRAY, BUT I REMEMBERED YOU.

—and now I return longing and thirsting for your fountain.

I MYSELF CANNOT GIVE LIFE.

OF MYSELF I HAVE LIVED WRONGLY;

IN YOU I HAVE FOUND LIFE AGAIN.

—and now I return longing and thirsting for your fountain.

TE DEUM

(On Sundays, except in Lent, and on Feasts and Solemnities.)

YOU ARE GOD: WE PRAISE YOU;

You are the Lord: we acclaim you;
You are the eternal Father:
All creation worships you.

To you all angels, all the powers of heaven,
Cherubim and Seraphim, sing in endless praise:
   Holy, holy, holy, Lord, God of power and might,
   heaven and earth are full of your glory.

The glorious company of apostles praise you.
The noble fellowship of prophets praise you.
The white-robed army of martyrs praise you.

Throughout the world the holy Church acclaims you:
Father, of majesty unbounded,
your true and only Son, worthy of all worship,
and the Holy Spirit, advocate and guide.

You, Christ, are the king of glory,
the eternal Son of the Father.
When you became man to set us free

you did not spurn the Virgin's womb.
You overcame the sting of death,
and opened the kingdom of heaven to all believers.

You are seated at God's right hand in glory.
We believe that you will come, and be our judge.

Come then, Lord, and help your people,
Bought with the price of your own blood,
And bring us with your saints
To glory everlasting.

℣. Save your people, Lord, and bless your inheritance.
℟. Govern and uphold them now and always.

℣. Day by day we bless you.
℟. We praise your name for ever.

℣. Keep us today, Lord, from all sin.
℟. Have mercy on us, Lord, have mercy.

℣. Lord, show us your love and mercy;
℟. for we put our trust in you.

℣. In you, Lord, is our hope:
℟. and we shall never hope in vain.

FINAL PRAYER

LET US PRAY.

LORD, RENEW IN YOUR CHURCH THE SPIRIT YOU GAVE SAINT AUGUSTINE. FILLED WITH THIS SPIRIT, MAY WE THIRST FOR YOU ALONE AS THE FOUNTAIN OF WISDOM AND SEEK YOU AS THE SOURCE OF ETERNAL LOVE.

WE ASK THIS THROUGH OUR LORD JESUS CHRIST, YOUR SON, WHO LIVES AND REIGNS WITH YOU AND THE HOLY SPIRIT, ONE GOD, FOR EVER AND EVER. *Amen.*

SELECT BIBLIOGRAPHY

The Liturgy of the Hours

EDITIONS USED IN THIS BOOK:

Christian Prayer. New Jersey: Catholic Book Publishing Corp., 1976. 1 volume version.

The Liturgy of the Hours. New Jersey: Catholic Book Publishing Corp., 1975. 4 volumes.

RELATED TEXTS:

Baltzer, R.A. and Fassler, M.E. *The Divine Office in the Later Middle Ages. Studies in Honor of R. Steiner.* New York: Oxford University Press, 2000.

Bradshaw, P. *Daily Prayer in the Early Church: A Study of the Origin and Early Development of the Divine Office.* London: Alciun Club, 1981.

____. *Early Christian Worship, A Basic Introduction to Ideas and Practice.* Collegeville, MN: Liturgical Press, 2000.

Brook, John. *The School of Prayer: An Introduction to the Divine Office for All Christians.* Collegeville, MN: Liturgical Press, 1992.

Campbell, Stanislaus. *From Breviary to Liturgy of Hours: The Structural Reform of the Roman Office.* Collegeville, MN: Liturgical Press, 1995.

Chrichton, James D. *Christian Celebration: The Prayer of the Church.* London: Chapman, 1976.

Dalmais, I.H., trans. M.J. O'Connell. *The Liturgy and Time.* Collegeville, MN: Liturgical Press, 1986.

Dix, G. *The Shape of the Liturgy.* London: Dacre Press, 1945.

Elliott, Peter J. *Ceremonies of the Modern Roman Rite: The Eucharist and the Liturgy of the Hours.* San Francisco: Ignatius Press, 1995.

Field, Anne, editor. *The Monastic Hours.* Collegeville, MN: Liturgical Press, 2001.

Guiver, George. *Company of Voices: Daily Prayer and the People of God.* New York: Pueblo, 1988.

Irwin, Kevin W. *Advent and Christmas: A Guide to the Eucharist and Hours.* New York: Pueblo, 1986.

____. *Context and Text: Method in Liturgical Theology.* Collegeville, MN: Liturgical Press, 1994.

____. *Easter: A Guide to the Eucharist and Hours.* Collegeville, MN: Liturgical Press, 1991.

____. *Lent: A Guide to the Eucharist and Hours.* New York: Pueblo, 1985.

Jurgens, W.A. *General Instruction in the Liturgy of the Hours.* Collegeville, MN: Liturgical Press, 1975.

Little, Vilma G. *The Sacrifice of Praise: An Introduction to the Meaning and Use of the Divine Office.* London: Longmans, Green and Co., 1957.

Nugent, Madeline Pecora. *The Divine Office for Dodos.* New Jersey: Catholic Book Publishing Corp., 2008.

Parsch, P., trans. W. Nayden and C. Hoegerl. *The Breviary Explained.* St. Louis: Herder, 1954.

Roquet, A.M., OP. *The Liturgy of the Hours.* London: G. Chapman, 1971.

Salmon, P. *The Breviary Through the Centuries.* Collegeville, MN: Liturgical Press, 1986.

Scotto, Dominic. *The Liturgy of the Hours: Its History and Importance as the Communal Prayer of the Church after the Liturgical Reform of Vatican II.* Petersham: St. Bede's Press, 1986.

Sullivan, Shirley. *A Companion to the Liturgy of the Hours, Morning and Evening Prayer.* New Jersey: Catholic Book Publishing Corp., 2004.

Taft, Robert. *The Liturgy of the Hours in East and West.* 2nd edition. Collegeville, MN: Liturgical Press, 1986.

Van Dijk, S.J.P., ed. *Sources of the Modern Roman Liturgy.* Leiden: E.J. Brill, 1963.

Van Dijk, S.J.P. and Walker, J.H. *The Origins of the Modern Roman Liturgy: The Liturgy of the Papal Court and the Franciscan Order in the Thirteenth Century.* London: Darton, Longman and Todd, 1960.

Zimmerman, Joyce A. *Morning and Evening: A Parish Celebration.* Chicago: Liturgy Training Publications, 1996.

709/13

LITURGY OF THE HOURS

This is the official English edition of the Divine Office that contains the translation approved by the International Committee on English in the Liturgy.

No. 409/10 Set of 4 volumes **155.00**
ISBN 978-0-89942-409-5

No. 409/13 Set of 4 volumes—Black Leather Binding
Note: available in sets only **179.00**
ISBN 978-0-89942-411-8

No. 709/13 Set of 4 volumes—Large-print, Leather Binding. *Note: available in sets only* **199.00**
ISBN 978-0-89942-710-2

ACTUAL SIZE TYPE

READING

I know well the plans I have
Lord, plans for your welfare, n
you a future full of hope. When

409/10

409/13

406/10
406/23
407/10

CHRISTIAN PRAYER

Here are the official one-volume editions of the new internationally acclaimed "Liturgy of the Hours." These new versions contain the complete texts of Morning and Evening Prayer for the entire year. The large-type edition is ideal for those with difficulty in reading. It has the same pagination as the regular edition.

No. 406/10—Regular Ed.—Flex. Maroon cover....... **37.95**
ISBN 978-0-89942-406-4

No. 406/23—Regular Ed.—Zipper binding **46.00**
ISBN 978-0-89942-424-8

No. 407/10—Large Type Ed. Flex. Maroon cover...... **39.00**
ISBN 978-0-89942-407-1

CHRISTIAN PRAYER LEATHER ZIPPER CASES

No. 406/13LC—Christian Prayer leather zipper case
ISBN 978-1-937913-41-0 .... **19.95**

No. 407/10LC—Christian Prayer leather zipper case for Large Type Edition
ISBN 978-1-937913-42-7 .... **22.95**

www.catholicbookpublishing.com

SHORTER CHRISTIAN PRAYER

Contains Morning and Evening Prayer from the Four Week Psalter and selected texts for the Seasons and Major Feasts of the year. It is ideal for Parish use.

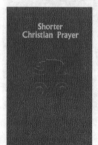

No. 418/10—Large Type Edition Flexible Maroon cover **19.95**
ISBN 978-0-89942-453-8

No. 408/10—Pocket Edition Flexible Maroon cover **15.95**
ISBN 978-0-89942-408-8

DAYTIME PRAYER

Composed of prayers for midmorning, midday and midafternoon. The inidividual may use all three or select the one set of prayers most suitable for the occasion or the hour of the day. Suitable for both individual and group use. A selection of of hymns is provided as well as a complementary psalmody for those who pray more than one of the Daytime Prayers. Printed in two colors.

No. 422/10—Flexible cover..**11.95**
ISBN 978-0-89942-454-5

A COMPANION TO THE LITURGY OF THE HOURS: MORNING AND EVENING PRAYER

Shirley Darcus Sullivan

A spiritual companion that presents ways in which the experience of the Hours may be made more prayerful for those who say them, e.g., by using the spirituality of Carmel, especially that of Elizabeth of the Trinity. 208 pages. Size 5¹/₂ x 8¹/₄.

No. 415/04—Flexible cover **8.95**
ISBN 978-0-89942-432-3